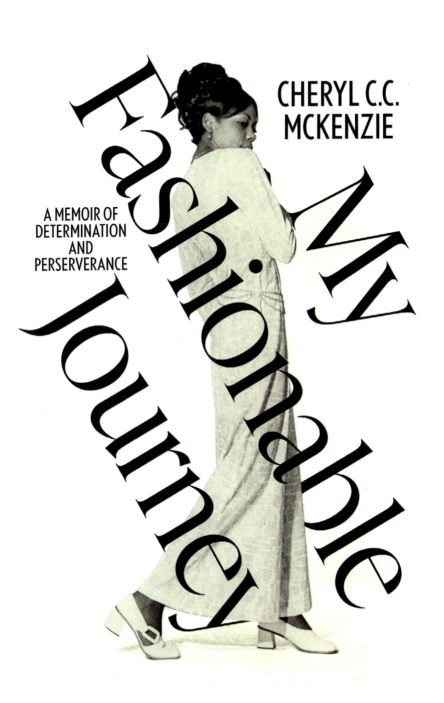

CHERYL C.C.
MCKENZIE

A MEMOIR OF
DETERMINATION
AND
PERSERVERANCE

My Fashionable Journey

My Fashionable Journey: A Memoir of Determinination and Perseverance

Copyright©2022 Cheryl McKenzie

ISBN: 978-1-66783-567-9 (softcover)

Author: Cheryl C.C. McKenzie

Layout & Cover Design: BookBaby

Publisher: BookBaby

Printed in the United States

This book is dedicated to my younger sister, Marie Alethia Rose McKenzie. Your untimely passing snatched you from Earth on April 20, 2020, nine days before your 72nd birthday.

To my grandmother, Corinne, whose design, and exemplary sewing skills inspired and fueled my start in fashion.

And

To Saint Rose, a follower of Mother Teresa, who left us this principle of living a simple life, who gave so much and asked for nothing in return.

—Cheryl

The Lord is my shepherd, I shall not want.

—Psalm 23

Acknowledgements

Writing a memoir is more challenging than I expected; the experience has been rewarding, as deep-set family values made me better understand who I am and who I am meant to be! I was reminded of things about myself that still exist. Discovering my true self would not have been possible without taking time to recall past memories.

Thank you to my older sister Claudette for reminders of our growing up together and taking time jogging our not-so-young minds of dates, events, and childhood memories of fun times with family members in grandma's rose gardens. The legacy of our Jamaican family history and heritage.

To my daughter Mackenzie, my heart beat who kept encouraging me to tell my story, and for giving me the space to recreate laughter and fun times we had while you were growing up in Queens, New York.

Last but surely not least, thank God for giving me strength, grace, and power to do all things through his love and blessings.
Praise be to God.

Contents

Introduction

Sitting at the round, gray, wooden table with its four matching chairs and beige padded seating in the nook at my daughter Mackie's home in Mardela Springs, Maryland, I gazed at the freshly manicured lawn of green grass and listened to the birds noisily chirping. This scene brought back vibrant memories of my childhood and family interactions growing up on the island of Jamaica in the West Indies during the 1950s.

I lived with my mother, Gertrude, my father Jasper, and two sisters, Claudette, and Marie, in a small brick house on Fleet Street in downtown Kingston. Claudette was the firstborn, I was the middle sibling, and Marie was the third sibling, usually referred to as the baby.

My mother, Gertrude, was a Licensed Practical Nurse and a midwife who delivered newborn babies at the homes of soon-to-be mothers, who requested her service instead of going to the local hospital. During the 1950s, my mother left home very early in the morning to catch the bus for work at Mona Rehabilitation Center hospital during the Polio epidemic in Jamaica. My father Jasper operated his own tailoring business in downtown Kingston, creating stylish one-of-a-kind men's three-piece suits, complete with pants, vest, and matching jacket. He was an impeccable dresser, ensuring that his clothing always fit his lean and slender body frame.

My parents would take the 20-minute drive from Kingston to Saint Andrew to leave us at our grandparents' house on Mountain View Avenue, so my grandmother could provide childcare for us while both of my parents worked. Sometimes our visits would extend into the weekend, which excited us, as Grandma would serve her favorite Sunday special of fried chicken, rice and peas, fried plantains, and homemade vanilla ice cream for dessert. However, when it was time for us to start going to school, Mom moved to Mountain View Avenue to live at Grandma's house, as it was more convenient for us to attend school in Saint Andrew, closer to our grandparents' home, and for my mother to go to work in Mona.

As we children called her our grandmother or mamma, Corinne was a housewife and a dressmaker who would cut freehand without using a pattern. Instead, she'd create her design from a cotton floral print fabric and then sew the most beautiful dresses for my sisters and me, with a white crinoline underlay made out of a fine mesh type fabric to keep the wide skirt billowing from our tiny waists.

She was also a good cook and an excellent baker. During the Christmas holidays, the raisins, and currants, which had been soaking in a large jar of fine port wine all year, would be removed from the pantry shelving in preparation for Christmas baking. She would place the ingredients in a large mixing bowl. We would patiently wait for her to scrape the mixture into the baking pans, leaving just enough of the delicious residue in the bowl for us to swirl our fingers around the edges, catching the leftover dough mix and placing it into our mouths. You could smell the aroma coming from her kitchen as she baked her Christmas fruit cake.

Benjamin, our granddad, was a quiet man. He loved working with numbers and was efficient with financial management. He worked as an accountant for a Syrian company in Kingston, making a good salary that allowed Grandma to remain at home taking care of the grandchildren when needed.

Daniel, my mother's only brother, was the youngest and worked as a civil servant for the Jamaican government at the House of Representatives on Duke Street in downtown Kingston. He was the brain in the family and earned a full scholarship to Oxford University in London, England. After returning to Jamaica, he and his wife Barbara migrated to Hope, British Colombia, Canada. In addition, my aunts Ruth and Beatrice who were also civil servants, migrated to the United Kingdom early in their careers.

Living in Jamaica presented the challenge of finding a skilled or a professional job immediately after graduating high school, as there were more applicants than available job openings. During the summer holidays, I was fortunate to have a job at the Bustamante Industrial Trade Union and the Water Commission in Kingston. I learned customer service skills and typed fifty words per minute while working at both positions. Before I graduated from Immaculate Conception High School in 1965, I took secretarial skills classes, where I learned how to operate different machines, including the IBM data entry machines.

The new skills I honed helped me to secure employment in New Kingston at Datatron, one of Jamaica's data entry firms, working as a data entry clerk after graduating high school. This job was the opportunity of a lifetime, as there was a waiting list of applicants, and only a few ever made it to being interviewed. The first day of work was scary, as I had to work in a room of 50 to 60 employees, all operating IBM machines. They stacked each device with blank cards measuring approximately 7 3/8 inches long by 3 1/4 inches high, with one of the upper corners cut at an angle. As I closely observed, the cards moved from one end of the machine to the opposite end while punching small holes, then stacking them in the output bin.

My first week of work was tedious. I took extensive notes and learned what the punched holes represented and how information was gathered electronically for company invoices, accounts payable, parking tickets, and vouchers requested from overseas firms. However, the job also presented a unique opportunity to work alongside employees from the United States who had been with the company for many years. I also assisted employees in Jamaica when challenges arose.

Listening to these overseas workers discuss life in the United States piqued my interest, as I learned there was a need for skilled workers. I listened attentively to their many stories about snow up to their waist in winter and the sun shining late into the evening in the summer. I was intrigued by this fact, as I was used to year-round summer. I would pepper them with all kinds of questions about life in the United States, and the more I heard, the more excited I became. I also heard that I would be eligible for two weeks' vacation if I stayed employed for one year at Datatron. With that goal in mind, I speedily scheduled an appointment with the United States Embassy in Jamaica to apply for a temporary visitor's visa to the United States. The process was long and arduous, but I was finally granted the two-week visitor's visa in 1967.

My two-week vacation was full of excitement. I thoroughly enjoyed shopping in the Big Apple - New York City, the city that never sleeps - eating pizza for the first time, riding the subway trains, and visiting skyscrapers like the Empire State Building, Chrysler Building, and Rockefeller Center in New York City. However, I was unfamiliar with the palpable energy and the hustle and bustle of people rushing to get on the subway, catch a bus, and even push someone out of their way to get a seat. As my two weeks concluded, I wondered to myself if I could live in a big city. Would I find employment? Would I get accustomed to the cold weather and survive through months of snow? That first visit gave me a bird's-eye view of life in the United States. I was eager and determined to prepare myself to take the plunge to move there permanently for what I believed would be a better life.

My journey to success began
with following the footsteps
of those who have gone before me!

CHAPTER 1

Guardian Angel

I can't believe no one came to the airport to meet me, I thought to myself after my plane from Jamaica landed at JFK international airport. I was shocked, stunned, and worried as I stood there waiting and watching the droves of people arriving on other flights. I stood there looking at the faces of every passenger and did not recognize anyone familiar. Not one person who had even a slight resemblance to any of my friends was in the airport as I wandered from bag carousel to bag carousel.

Anxious and bewildered, I walked back and forth to the arrival waiting area in the airport, wondering what would happen if no one came to pick me up. I had no contact information for my friends and only purchased a one-way ticket to the United States and did not have enough money for a return ticket for a flight back home to Jamaica.

When I returned to the baggage area, my luggage was the only one left on the carousel. I stood there watching it go round and round like a merry-go-round. The frown on my face was a dead giveaway of fear as a woman approached me and struck up a conversation. The woman told me that she had just returned from a vacation in Jamaica and had an enjoyable time. I told her I was Jamaican and would be living in the United States. I shared that I was waiting for friends to pick me up to go to Brooklyn.

By now, the airport was almost empty, and most passengers had gathered outside at the taxi stand waiting for service or standing on the side waiting for someone to pick them up. The look on my face must have concerned the woman, as it was evident that I was scared.

It now dawned on me that I was stranded! The woman asked me if I wanted to share a taxi, as she was going to Brooklyn. I felt helpless as I replied that I did not have the address or the telephone number where my friends were staying or know how to get in touch with them. She looked at me, frowning.

"How are you going to get there? The taxi driver will need the address." Then, shaking her head, she said, "I don't want to leave you here."

I explained that I only purchased a one-way ticket to the United States.

"I can let you stay in my house for the night since it is getting quite late."

Fear gripped my stomach. I had just met the woman for the first time. I did not know how to respond. Could I trust the stranger, and why was she helping me? Who sent her to rescue me? I knew God was watching over me as this total stranger took a risk on a young Jamaican woman with nowhere to go.

We walked outside to the taxi stand. As the taxi driver approached us, she handed him her address. The driver placed our pieces of luggage in the trunk as we boarded the cab. During the drive to Brooklyn, I silently prayed for protection. I was taking a chance going with a stranger I met at the airport. I had no idea where the woman was taking me.

Me, modeling the three-piece pant suit
(PERSONAL COLLECTION OF CHERYL MCKENZIE)

Who is she? Is this my guardian angel?

While driving in the taxi to Brooklyn, she shared that her husband was in the United States Army, and she would put me up for the night but had to inform him in the morning because she did not want to worry him by having a stranger in the house. We arrived in Brooklyn along a well-lit street lined with three-story brownstone buildings. There were stoops on either side where people could meet and talk. This scenery reminded me of my home in Jamaica, except we only had the one-story ranch-style home with a veranda in the front and a chain-link fence with fresh green plant edging surrounding the entire yard, with a gate facing the front of the house for entering the yard.

My large, bright pink Samsonite luggage had me struggling under its heavyweight as I placed my feet one at a time in front of me in my quest to reach that final step. I closed my eyes and quietly thanked God for hearing my silent prayer asking for strength. The woman quickly made it to the top of the last step and opened the two locks on the large brown door with the decorated glass in the center.

She placed her back against the door to keep it ajar, beckoning me to follow her inside before bolting the door behind her with a snap of the top lock and the next lock below, making sure it was securely closed.

I entered a spacious living room exquisitely decorated with a sofa and two leather armchairs, with a large coffee table in the center. The window drapes added an elegant ambiance to the room. I stood still as my eyes landed on the fireplace. I had never before seen a fireplace in a house. In Jamaica, we only had open fires in the back yard when burning dried bushes or twigs or sometimes garbage. I continued my gaze to the mantel with the nicely decorated runner, on which sat glass ornaments and a clear candy jar filled with candy.

The dining room was furnished with a large brown wooden table and had six chairs with padded seating. It was next to the living room. There was also a curio or china cabinet with drinking glasses, colorful cups, and saucers.

The woman showed me to a bedroom next to the bathroom. As I was settling, I was startled at the *bam, bam, bam* on the door. The woman opened the door and entered to ensure I did not need anything, as she was ready for bed. The other bedroom was on the other side of the bathroom that separated both bedrooms and gave both occupants privacy.

Restless, I tossed and turned through the daunting and endless night as I missed my home and the comfortable bed in St. Andrew, Jamaica. The woman had already left the apartment for work when I awoke that morning. She left me a note on the fridge, reminding me for the second time not to open the door for anyone and not to leave the house.

How could I leave the house? I had no keys. Yet somehow, I believed that this woman was my guardian angel, and our paths crossed for a reason.

After a large bowl of cold cereal for breakfast, I returned to my bedroom to get some items from my luggage. I did not see my passport while going through the small luggage with my personal belongings. I recalled placing it there before boarding the taxi. I searched the large bags and my handbag. Unfortunately, there was no passport. I panicked, as this was the only legal document I had to prove my entry into the United States. I did not know what I would do if it were lost.

Hearing a ring from the telephone, I went to the living room, walked across the floor to the small table in the corner, and picked up the receiver. With my hand shaking, I said,

"Hello."

I sat on the sofa to settle my nervousness. As I was not expecting a call, I sat quietly for a couple of seconds. The caller on the other end told me there was a message left on the fridge. Then I realized the woman had called to check on me.

I told her I could not find my passport. Again, there was silence on the other end of the phone. Then, finally, she apologized and acknowledged she had mistakenly taken the paper shopping bag, not knowing that my US passport was at the bottom of the bag.

"I will return it to you when I get home from work."

As I remained seated on the sofa, the conversation ended quickly. I wondered if this was the beginning of setbacks to discourage me.

You never know who will show up
when you need help.

CHAPTER 2

Locating Friends

During the first couple of days at my guardian angel's home, I was more comfortable sticking to the daily routine of waking up at 10 am and going to bed at 9 pm. With nothing much to occupy my time during the day, I made plans to accomplish the next goal of locating my friends.

The woman shared that she expected her husband home on leave in a couple of weeks. With this new information, I was now more determined to find my friends, hoping to be gone before he returned home.

Luckily, I had the contact information of another friend, who was also a friend of the friends with whom I was to share the apartment in Brooklyn. So, I reached out to that friend by telephone and asked for help locating my future housemates, sharing contact information on how to reach me.

As the weekend approached, I was worried about not hearing from my friends. Furthermore, I was perplexed, as I had little money and no job, nor had I informed my family of my whereabouts. Then, around 5 pm on Sunday, I received a telephone call.

One of my friends told me how worried they had been about not hearing from me. They may have forgotten that I had no way of contacting them, as they had not given me the contact information. I reminded them of our last conversation about picking me up at the airport. All I knew was that they were living in Brooklyn.

I said very little during the conversation, as I did not discuss my living situation. Finally, feeling frustrated, I hastily bid goodbye and ended the conversation. I immediately left the living room. My guardian angel was in the kitchen preparing dinner as I communicated my plan to leave at the end of the following week before her husband arrived home.

The day to leave my guardian angel's home arrived, and as I waved goodbye from the taxi, I was sad and began to miss the ambiance of a comfortable home provided to me over a couple of weeks. Yet I was grateful that God protected me by answering my prayers when I had nowhere to go.

On my first visit back home to Jamaica, I shared my tragedy with my family and recalled hearing my sisters whispering, "I would have taken the next flight back to Jamaica."

Yeah, I thought, *easier said than done,* as no other planes were leaving the airport for that night. So I would have had to spend the night at the airport.

So many years have passed, and to this day, I cannot remember the name of the kind stranger whom I call my guardian angel, but I am grateful for her kindness.

Never put all your eggs in one basket.

CHAPTER 3

Living With Friends

The reality of living in the United States gave me an adrenaline rush as I danced around my room with glee. Finally, I now could live out my fantasy of attending basement parties in Brooklyn where eligible single men would line the walls of the dance floor as they eye-rolled and checked the women, planning which one they were going to take home that night. I visualized boat rides up the Hudson River in Manhattan with reggae and calypso music blasting in the background, making me even more excited. There was no stopping me now, as I was here to start a new life for myself.

Visualize five young ladies living in a three-bedroom apartment on the third floor of a ten-story building in Brooklyn. The apartment we all shared was large, spacious, and affordable. The rent and utilities were divided evenly amongst the five people living there. I supported my end of the agreement for my share of the rent, although I was not employed. Looking for work was non-stop. As the other four ladies were employed, I became eager to begin work and collect an American paycheck.

One of the ladies had a visiting boyfriend, who was asked to pick me up at the airport that dreadful and unforgettable night I arrived from Jamaica, West Indies. I will never forget the kindness of a stranger whose name I have forgotten over the years and who I call my guardian angel.

Moving to my new place became the beginning of a new chapter in my life, and I was determined to succeed with the goals I set before migrating to the United States.

My efforts in pounding the streets looking for work paid off. I soon landed a job through a temporary agency in Manhattan and kept looking for full-time employment. Finally, I gained a full-time position at Texaco Company in Manhattan shortly after working part-time.

While still living with friends, I decided to look for an apartment in Brooklyn, becoming familiar with the neighborhood. With the help of a rental agency, I found a one-bedroom apartment in a two-story private house in Flatbush, Brooklyn. Unfortunately, my housemates had no idea that I had found a new place to live. After sharing the news with them and bidding my housemates and roommate goodbye, I hailed a taxi to my new home. It would be the last time I set my eyes on these friends who left me stranded at the airport.

In the beginning, my situation was not ideal, as it was difficult being in a new place. I quickly adjusted to living alone, although money was tight. I had to seek additional employment to cover my rent and living expenses. I have never regretted my choice to live on my own. My focus was on becoming a fashion designer. My pursuit of success was apparent, and I ensured that nothing would stand in my way. I had to strike out on my own to accomplish other goals.

My first goal was to become a fashion designer in New York and operate my own business. I learned the valuable skill of making beautiful dresses from my grandmother Corinne, but I lacked the training and skills needed to design, complete, and grade patterns into various sizes.

Me, modeling the jumpsuit all in one garment in my early twenties
(PERSONAL COLLECTION OF CHERYL MCKENZIE)

Our steps in life are divinely ordered.
Therefore, what is to be will be.

CHAPTER 4

Employment

I continued working at Texaco while working part-time in the evenings. I learned I could save extra money by renting an apartment in Queens instead of Brooklyn. Being single had its perks and its drawbacks, as I could only depend on myself if I planned to survive.

Yet before I could have any more thoughts, my favorite Jamaican reggae artist Bob Marley's song came on the radio singing, "Don't worry, everything's gonna be all right." A smile crossed my lips. I was confident I would succeed if I continued to keep my eyes on the prize. Then my purpose in coming to the United States would take place.

My effort to fit my American lifestyle into the daily routine of a Monday to Friday work week was easy, as I was accustomed to working a 9 am to 5 pm schedule. However, I had two jobs, and the hindrance of cold weather and snow complicated my travel, especially when I had early morning assignments. Although balancing a full-time job and two part-time jobs were challenging, I needed to keep a roof over my head and save enough money to one day move to Queens.

So, my Thursday night disco dancing and basement parties were put on hold.

After some time and before moving to Jamaica, Queens, in 1972, I resigned from my job at Texaco and began working at the National Broadcasting Corporation (NBC), located at 30 Rockefeller Plaza in New York City.

During my two-week vacation, I visited Rockefeller Plaza and was intrigued by the height of the building. I worked on the 12th floor of the 68-floor skyscraper. What I remembered most was the elevator attendant explaining that the elevator bypassed the 13th floor as there were no tenants on that floor. Unfortunately, I never really understood the superstitious reasoning behind his explanation.

I worked in the payroll office, key-punching data on the same type of IBM machine I used in Jamaica, West Indies. While at work and just before lunch, my pocketbook went missing one day. I was the only one in the office on that day. I had just left to go to the ladies' room. Security came to my rescue, searched the entire floor, including the emergency exit door, and found my pocketbook behind the door with my money missing. Thank God the thief left one credit card, my ID, and house keys.

My fondest memory while working at NBC was visiting the commissary, a store where employees could purchase electronic items and pay for them with bi-weekly payroll deductions. I bought my first RCA-brand television in the United States from the commissary.

Radio City Music Hall, home of the world-famous Radio City Rockettes, was located near NBC. The Rockettes performed a Christmas Spectacular for young and old, dazzling theatre-goers with sparkling costumes, beautiful smiles, and high kicks each year. It is a show I still look forward to seeing each year. But, of course, my favorite activity is walking along 5th Avenue during the holiday season, looking at the beautifully decorated store windows.

The move to Jamaica, Queens, in 1972 proved heartbreaking. I was now leaving friendships and business relationships formed over my ten years in Brooklyn. Traveling to Brooklyn on the weekend was chaotic, even if you had a car. My weekly hairdresser appointment became a bi-weekly visit, as I now had to work every other Saturday. Brooklyn had the best hairdressers, and most of them could press and curl like the ones in Jamaica. Most African Americans would either relax their hair and sit under the burning hot dryer with rollers or hot press their hair with a pressing iron, then use a heated curling iron. They could style your hair with such perfection, leaving your hair looking like a movie star.

The commute from Queens to NBC took the same amount of time I would travel from Brooklyn. I now could look forward to getting a seat on the subway as I boarded the subway at the first stop going to work. Now returning home was another story. So, wearing comfortable shoes helped as there was no guarantee of getting a seat on the subway.

Moving to Queens supported my perception of the quality of life I dreamed of before moving to the United States. Less crowded streets, beautiful shopping centers and malls, and diverse cultures reminded me of life in Jamaica, living among different types of people in my community of Hampstead Park in Saint Andrew.

I learned early that one job could not support the life I envisioned; on the other hand, having too many part-time jobs was detrimental to my health. Since arriving in the United States, all my part-time and full-time positions have been data entry. Once I decided to move, the day to orchestrate my move to Jamaica, Queens, finally arrived, and I was leaving Brooklyn for good. I was happy as a lark!

It's good to dream,
but a dream without following a plan
falls short in accomplishing the goal.

CHAPTER 5

Back to School

*W*hy *do you want to go back to school? Are you crazy?* I asked myself. Would I have enough money to pay tuition and school fees? I pondered both questions, and the thought kept resurfacing, but I was determined to find a way to make it happen for me. I spent hours combing through college admission materials and newspaper advertisements, looking for a college that would fit my needs. Finally, I found two schools in New York City. I filled out the admission application for Parson School of Design, a private four-year college, and Fashion Institute of Technology, a two-year public college.

After mailing the applications, I shared the news with Marie, my younger sister, during our regular weekend chat. During the telephone conversation, I elaborated on my intent to quit my job and attend school full-time to study fashion design. Marie has been the biggest supporter of my many ideas. Although she appears to be entirely satisfied, she was employed by Georgie Girls temporary agency for many years working for Barclays Bank in New York City before landing a full-time position. She worked for over three decades before retiring in 2010.

Surprisingly, my older sister Claudette, who resides in Florida, was ecstatic and encouraged me to continue mamma's legacy as a dressmaker. "My dream was not just to become a dressmaker but a New York fashion designer." The acknowledgments meant so much to me as my ultimate goal was to become a successful designer and own a fashion design business. However, I knew that I would persevere as I continued to do what my sister Marie suggested: "Just pray about it."

My prayer was answered when Parsons School of Design was the first to respond, but unfortunately not the answer I expected. My admission application was rejected. As I reviewed the reason for the rejection, I was disappointed and took the letter, rolled it into a ball, and tossed it into the empty garbage can by the mailboxes in the lobby. I was angry and upset but reminded myself that I could not afford the tuition even if accepted.

Returning to my first-floor apartment, I decided not to lose hope, knowing that I had not received a response from the Fashion Institute of Technology (FIT), the other school where I applied. With my fingers crossed, I held onto hope. I waited daily for a response from FIT. Each day I would rush to the mailbox, hoping to receive a response. Finally, the answer arrived as a pre-acceptance letter. I was going to be a student at FIT!

Wait ~ the pre-acceptance letter was contingent on submitting additional documentation and an interview with the admission committee before the final decision. In addition, I had to take the placement test and prepare to present a portfolio of my work, including a garment that was designed and sewed by me. I was also expected to sketch and give my idea on paper during the interview with a team of three FIT professors. My preparation and hard work paid off when I received my acceptance letter in the mail to begin classes in the spring of 1975.

The first day of school finally arrived. I was up early and eager to start my new journey of becoming a fashion designer. I purchased my oversize black portfolio and decided to take it with me on the first day of school, as I was proud to be a FIT student.

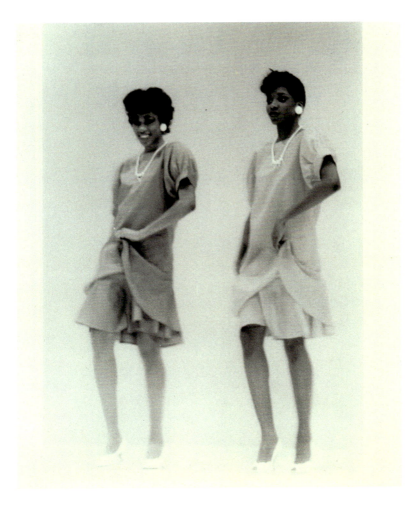

Doubletake - Swirling into Spring, 1984
(PERSONAL COLLECTION OF CHERYL MCKENZIE)

Model wearing two-tiered off-white dress
(PERSONAL COLLECTION OF CHERYL MCKENZIE)

After exiting the subway at 23rd Street and 7th Avenue in New York City, I walked four blocks to 27th Street, making sure to sit in the last car of the subway to prevent walking an extra block to the college. I arrived at my first class and chose a seat in the back of the classroom, as other students already took most seats upfront. Looking around the room, I observed students' interactions and felt like a fish out of water. They looked young and fresh out of high school. Some were standing, while others sat on their desks as we waited for the instructor to arrive. As I watched them laughing and chatting with each other, I wondered if I had made a mistake quitting my job to follow my dream. Well, there was no turning back as I was here on my first day of class, and the semester was eighteen weeks long.

As the semester progressed, the practical classes of draping, pattern making, and machine knitting were easy to grasp. My previous experience in choosing the correct fabric, cutting out the garment, and sewing the pieces together to complete the garment served me well.

Like many other students in the class room, I was eager to start sketching my ideas ~ one of the first steps in designing the many different types of garments. So naturally, the students were excited, as each one had to deliver an oral presentation of what their sketch represented, and the type of fabric used. Looking at the students' sketches who had gone before me, I thought mine was the worst, although I could confidently explain what I planned on making using the skills I learned from my grandmother back home in Jamaica. Yes, my explanation was fluid, although I was nervous when all eyes were on me as I stood in front of the class.

Students learned to create garments in the draping room; which was a regular classroom with mannequin figures, a large working table at the back of the room, and traditional students' desks. A lightweight piece of muslin cloth was draped on the mannequin dummy, with sewing machines and a cutting table in the draping room. The students were now creating and visualizing the finished garment by draping the muslin-like fabric on the form and manipulating the idea sketched, while using pins to hold the material in place. We then transferred the idea to paper to make the first pattern, which was usually a size 8 sample, and then upgraded to larger sizes based on the fashion's house name brand you were designing.

As I settled into the chair in front of the Singer industrial sewing machine, I was ready to put the skills I learned from Mamma to the test. I remember hearing her sewing machine engine zipping along with the tap of her feet and the speed of her hand turning the wheel to start the process. Under Mamma's guidance in Jamaica, years of sewing gave me a head start with my garment training. The theory classes presented a challenge, but the practical classes were a breeze, and I excelled because of my sewing experience. Nevertheless, I hung in there, and as I was only working part-time, I had extra time to remain at school, spending long hours in the library to keep my grades up to keep my financial aid.

The two years went by quickly, and before long I graduated with my degree in Fashion Design. However, I was not ready to leave the comfort of FIT and decided to continue my education by applying to the Fine Arts program there as well. During those additional two years, I honed my jewelry, hat, and shoe design skills, but I always kept my goal of being a fashion designer, not an accessory designer.

After earning my four-year degree, reality set in. Seeking a job in the fashion industry was more complicated than I expected. I learned that even if you had a job, you never knew if you would still have a job by the end of the week.

In 1979 Judi C. and I were discovered by Eartha Kitt, who was starring in Timbuktu's hit Broadway show. We put out designing skills to the test and presented a line of spring and summer clothing for the fashion-conscious at Stouffers on Chestnut Street in Philadelphia.

One of my highlights was collaborating with the designer Judi C., creating a complete ensemble, including a full-length rose-pink silk gown with a cowl neckline in the front, accessorized with a headpiece replicating the hibiscus flower on the bottle of Bon Chance perfume. This perfume was launched in 1979 by Flori Roberts Incorporated for the Fragrance Foundation's annual event. Meeting Eartha Kitt and her daughter Kitt, the model, was the second highlight of that evening.

My fashion design experience included working for several fashion companies. One of my tasks was cutting the pieces of the fabric for workers to produce complete garments. However, the pattern maker and design assistant positions were not close to what I envisioned working in the fashion industry. My experiences spanned in many directions, but the most rewarding was working for designer Miya Gowdy at the Seventh Avenue Utopia located in the Art Deco building on West 35th Street. In 1980 the editor for the Daily News wrote a unique feature on the fashion empire. In the article, I was featured working alongside Miya and one of her models.

You never know by whom,
by what, or how you will be inspired.
So never give up hope.

The following photos are from
the personal collection
of Cheryl C.C. McKenzie

Women tailored 2-piece business garments

Seventh Avenue Utopia

by CONSTANCE ROSENBLUM

Ask for Miya on the wrong floor of the Art Deco building at 264 W. 35th Street and you meet only blank stares. "We ain't got no Miya," announces the grubby workman who presides over the gray-on-gray operation on the fourth floor. "But we got a Mel. You wan'a Mel?"

No. We want Miya (pronounced MEE-ah) Gowdy, who runs a small dress business on the ninth floor of the building. And between Miya and Mel, there's all the difference in the world.

Judging by appearances, Mel runs a highly traditional operation, whereas Miya presides over what has the trappings of a little Utopian community. What's more, Mel, as far as we know, runs a comfortably for-profit business; with Miya it's touch and go and may be for some time.

Even the setting tells you this is no ordinary rag shop. Miya's space is large and sunny, set off by spanking black and white floor tile and a profusion of avocado trees grown from pit and

Constance Rosenblum is Special Features editor for the Daily News.

named for various workers—a Bob for partner Bob Van Bruggen, Gilbert for the master tailor. Beneath a mobile, a worker sips Chinese tea from a flowered mug.

If the workspace has the look of an oversized playroom, Miya herself resembles an overgrown child—dark feathery hair, wide-set gray eyes, crooked teeth, a voice that trembles on the edge of a giggle. She's 35, but you'd never guess.

What Miya has been running in this sun-splashed setting since last June is part cooperative, part cottage industry. Basically, she wants to preside over a dress business where workers have a say in what goes on, where punching a time clock isn't the day's most important chore, where profits—if and when—eventually trickle back to the staff.

It sounds terrific on paper; the reality is a little less glowing. For one thing, running a business doesn't always let you play Lady Bountiful. "I have compassion in my heart," says Miya with a rueful smile. "But sometimes in the heat of battle, I go crazy."

Besides, Utopias don't necessarily turn a profit. Miya has already lost tens of thousands of dollars just learning the nuts and bolts of the

industry. If she doesn't make it this season—and she might not—she could wind up just another statistic in the record books of a high-risk industry. On the other hand, she just might succeed, providing one more piece of evidence that the workplace doesn't have to be a jungle after all.

For starters, Miya has placed design and production activities under a single roof so workers can see how they fit into the total operation, have a chance to learn and, so Miya hopes, produce a better product. If, for example, Rea the sewing machine operator can't execute a detail that Cheryl the design assistant has proposed, the two can thrash out the problem on the spot.

Miya's hope is that the close relationship between design and production will result in stricter quality control, so the pieces she ships to stores like Bendel's and Ann Taylor, two New York shops that carry her line, will be as impeccably tailored as the snappy samples hanging in her office.

The firm's spring line—its first complete one, with 35 pieces—features mix and matchable skirts, pants, jackets and dresses that fall basically into the dress-for-success

Miya Gowdy meets buyers in the casual, airy showroom, above, where samples of her spring line are displayed and modeled.

Seventh Avenue Utopia- Miya Goudy
and Company buyers showroom, 1980

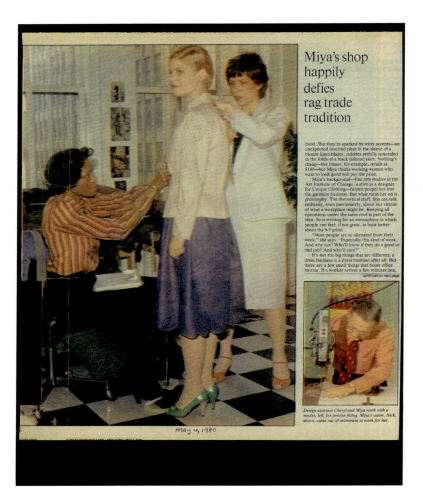

Miya's shop happily defies rag trade tradition

mold. But they're sparked by witty accents—an unexpected inverted pleat in the sleeve of a bronze linen blazer, culottes artfully concealed in the folds of a black tailored skirt. Nothing's cheap—the blazer, for example, retails at $180—but Miya thinks working women who want to look good will pay the price.

Miya's background—fine arts studies at the Art Institute of Chicago, a stint as a designer for Unique Clothing—helped propel her into the garment business. But what turns her on is philosophy. The theoretical stuff. She can talk endlessly, even passionately, about her visions of what a workplace might be. Keeping all operations under the same roof is part of the idea. So is striving for an atmosphere in which people can feel, if not great, at least better about the 9-5 grind.

"Most people are so alienated from their work," she says. "Especially this kind of work. And why not? Who'll know if they do a good or bad job? And who'll care?"

It's not the big things that are different; a dress business is a dress business after all. But there are a few small things that boost office morale. If a worker arrives a few minutes late,

continued on next page

Design assistant Cheryl and Miya work with a model, left, for precise fitting. Miya's cutter, Nick, above, came out of retirement to work for her.

MAY 4, 1980

Cheryl, design assistant fitting a model wearing a sample garment, 1980

Model dressed for cruising up the Hudson River on a boat ride

Dressed for success-Spring to Summer 1985

Spring ready - Soul Fashion show at FIT, 1984

Full size model - Soul Fashion show at FIT, 1984

From the men's wear collection - Soul Fashion show at FIT, 1984

Doubletake Soul Fashion show at Fashion Institute of Technology, 1984

Dressing for Success

Miss Guyana - New York Caribbean beauty pageant

Miss Haiti - New York Caribbean beauty pageant

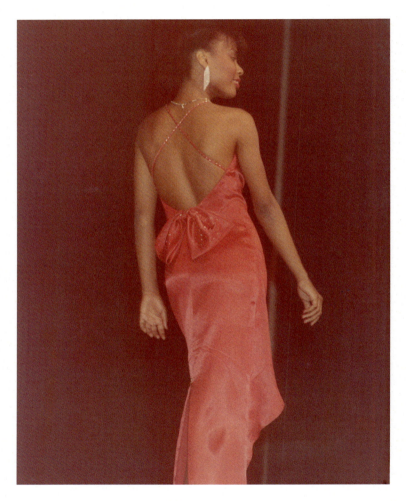

Miss Haiti strikes a pose, New York Caribbean beauty pageant

Beauty contestant with the winning personality and smile

Salute to the Armed Forces, Critics award – Soul Fashion Show at FIT 1984

Salute to the Armed Forces, Critics award - Soul Fashion Show at FIT, 1984

New York Caribbean beauty pageant – Miss Haiti national costume

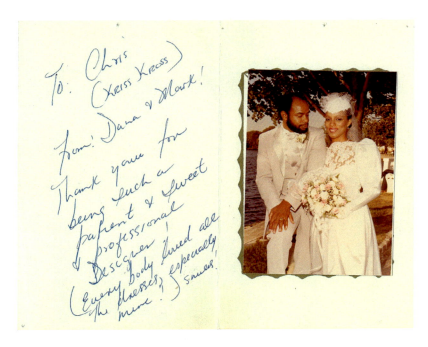

To: Chris
(Xriss Kross)

From: Dana & Mark!

Thank you for
being such a
patient & sweet
Designer & professional
(Everybody loved all
the dresses, especially
mine!) smiles!

Satisfied customer, bride wearing a dress designed by Cheryl McKenzie

Model wearing two-piece Bridal Jumpsuit with over-skirt

Model wearing Rhinestone (applied by hand) two-piece evening wear

CHAPTER 6

Courage

My long-term goal was to own a fashion design studio in New York City. However, my experience working for many fashion companies solidified my passion for designing couture one-of-a-kind garments for customers who want to be the best dressed at every event.

I obsessed over and over, visualizing customers scheduling appointments for personalized styles only for that individual, in the manner Corinne, my grandma in Jamaica, West Indies, serviced her clients.

Having just one more class to complete before earning a Bachelor's Degree in Fine Arts did not stop me from looking for a suitable place to rent. So in 1981, I began searching for small space for the design studio. I would stop at rental offices, pop in and out of designer buildings, and comb through rental advertisements in the newspaper, looking for a suitable loft space. I was familiar with the Chelsea fashion district and hoped to find rental space there. Unfortunately, it was frustrating and exhausting, as spaces I looked at were either too large or appeared to be overpriced. Nevertheless, I was determined to open a fashion design studio, so I kept looking.

Finally, I earned my Bachelor of Fine Arts degree and had more leverage when looking for design jobs. I was not fortunate to find a job in the industry and accepted the first job offer working for Zayre clothing warehouse in Chelsea. The scarcity of design jobs for new graduates left me no choice, as I needed to keep a roof over my head and save enough money as a deposit for my design studio.

My days were hectic and uninspiring, leaving my apartment in Jamaica, Queens at 8:30 am to catch the train to arrive in Manhattan by 10 am. The first item on my to-do list was stopping at the rental agency to check on leads. After walking and viewing spaces by noon, it was time for lunch. I would grab a slice of pizza with extra cheese or a McDonald's cheeseburger and fries. This routine occurred three days out of the week as I searched for a suitable place.

At 3 pm, I began my walk on the long blocks to my evening job at Zayre to arrive and punch in at 4 pm. Workers were docked if they came after 4 pm. So when it was time to check out, I would see workers already standing at the time clock at 10:59, waiting to punch out at 11 pm, then walk swiftly to exit.

The walk to the subway station was a couple of blocks through the dark and poorly lit streets of 10th Avenue and 23rd Street. I had to walk fast so I was not left behind. You just never knew if you would come face-to-face with a homeless person or get a scare from a rodent searching for food in the garbage.

When the subway trains ran on schedule, I arrived home at midnight, exhausted but thankful to be "home sweet home." Most nights, I would see one or two passengers who lived in my building on the train, so I had company walking the two blocks to my apartment. If not, I had to muster up the courage to walk home alone. I reminisce about fun times with my friends and wonder how they are doing. Our paths never crossed since the last time I bid them goodbye.

Dressed for Success
(PERSONAL COLLECTION OF CHERYL MCKENZIE)

Not long afterward, my determination and perseverance paid off, as I had saved enough money to put a deposit on an eight hundred square foot loft space on the third floor at 236 West 27th Street. This space was ideal for the Kriss Kross Fashions design studio I envisioned. However, it took quite some time for the idea of ownership to sink in.

After leaving the deposit, paying one month rent and receiving the keys, I returned to survey the space before making any plans for a kickoff celebration. The studio needed to be set up before making a business announcement. The walls needed painting, and the floor required a fresh coat of paint. In addition, every piece of old fur in corners, under the cutting table, around the radiator, and near heating poles had to be removed and discarded.

This additional task added more work to my already unrealistic to-do list. I was doing this alone. I started the business with money saved from working the part-time job. I felt discouraged thinking of my current situation, as I had very little start-up money and was worried about what lay ahead.

On Saturday of the first weekend, I spent hours removing remnants of old fur, cleaning dirt from an unkempt place. I felt disgusted and thought, *what did I get myself into?* Halfway through the day Marie, my younger sister, and Helene, my cousin came by with a bag of cleaning products. They were excited to see the studio. They helped paint the walls and the ceiling, leaving me to clean the windows.

We worked past 9 pm and planned to return on Sunday to put on the finishing touches and remove the large black garbage bags filled to the brim with dusty old fur remnants.

The studio was beginning to sparkle, resembling a workable place ready to be furnished from a thrift shop in Brooklyn. One man's trash is another man's treasure.

Kriss Kross Fashions was officially open for business—the first-ever fashion design studio in front of the Fashion Institute of Technology on West 27th Street. This new design studio slowly garnered curiosity from the college community, and before long, the doorbell was put to good use. Its ringing broke the silence, and I was brought back to reality. Overjoyed, overwhelmed, and nervous, I waited patiently for the first client to walk through the door.

I learned bookkeeping, accounting and all the "money stuff," and how to run a business while budgeting on a shoestring. I had to learn fast if I intended to make it in this cutthroat, rag trade business.

The business was slowly beginning to pick up. The few orders I received would be enough to pay the following month's rent if accounts payable remain in the green!

I enjoyed working as a designer, walking to 42nd Street to look at fabric samples for clients, trying out new ways of honing my craft, and creating my brand as a couture designer—it was all part of the fashion business.

The clientele attracted to Kriss Kross Fashions were boutique owners in Soho, the Village and quaint little shops in downtown Brooklyn, and beauty pageant contestants. They came in all ages, sizes, and shapes and had one thing in common: They were fashion-conscious and always wanted to impress. They were willing to pay the cost for exquisite designs created exclusively to fit their needs.

The thrill of designing evening wear for beauty pageant contestants, mother of the year contestants, celebrity weddings, and end of the year fashion shows kept me busy and, on my toes, constantly attending meetings with clients or an appointment outside of the studio.

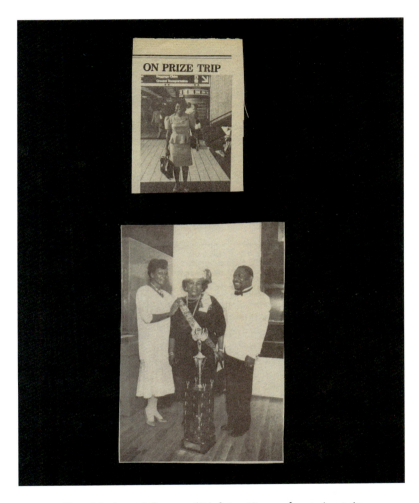

Top: Mother of the year '84 departing on her prize trip waring garment designed by Cheryl

Bottom: Mother of the year '85 with dress designer Cheryl and hat designer Carlos

As the information about the new designer in town, I began to receive acknowledgements of my presence and was featured in the local newspapers. I received requests to travel from New York state to as far as Nevada and parts of New York city. However, while exciting, other duties like working backstage during a fashion show with models and alongside other designers is considered part of designing and building relationship with people in the industry.

The fashion industry is fast-paced. The environment lends a atmosphere of a fun and lively encounters but at times becomes exhausting. Garments are created in advance before the each season begins as to have them ready for delivery to the stores. Clothing manufacturers are always busy, and designers who depend on a factory to sew their garments must build a good working relationship. Most small shops manufacture their garments in-house. Couture garments are usually created in-house from the beginning of the process to the end.

In 1983 Kriss Kross Fashions had an increase in its customer base. A client from the entertainment industry was interested in Kriss Kross garments. This led to a request in 1984, from R. J. Tobacco Company for Kriss Kross Fashions to participate in its annual competitive "More Fashion Awards" show. Although selected it was unfortunate that, Kriss Kross Fashions did not make the second round of selection and was invited back in 1985, a better year overall as they made the second round of selection. Although I did not win, the experience was electrifying to see my designs compete with other New York designers. It is something I will never forget.

The word spread like wild fire after the show and I was asked to design costumes for the ballroom scene in the dramatic musical, off-Broadway play *Keep Your Eyes to The Sky ~ It's Time for Coming Out*. This HS (Help Somebody) Production took place at Bank Street College Tabas Auditorium in West Harlem, New York. My life as a fashion designer was intriguing, electrifying, and satisfying. I accomplished my goal.

Easter Fashion Show, 1984
(PERSONAL COLLECTION OF CHERYL MCKENZIE)

Carib News Fashion Flash - Cheryl McKenzie aka Chris Kenzie, 1985

You never know who will cross your path
to lift you or to tear you down.

CHAPTER 7

Love and Trust

During the first three years after opening my design studio, I alone handled all areas of the small business, except sewing the garments. I had hired a part-time seamstress to sew. The studio opened at 10 am and closed at 3 pm to give me enough time to get to my evening job before 4 pm.

Managing the business and working a full-time job was strenuous. I was exhausted all the time and overworked. The two essential responsibilities, maintaining a roof over my head and running a design business, left me no choice if I planned on succeeding and accomplishing my goal. In addition, my passion for designing couture garments turned into a love for the fashion industry, leaving me little time for relationships.

In 1984, I traveled to Jamaica for a one-week vacation. The Saturday before I left Jamaica, some friends invited me to an event that included dancing. While on the dance floor, having a grand time and dancing up a storm, my movements caught the eye of a slim man perched up in a corner drinking a bottle of Red Stripe beer. Although he was not a good dancer, I had fun dancing most of the night. We exchanged numbers before leaving the dance floor, and I kept in touch for the next couple of months.

Our exchanges were primarily in writing and a few telephone calls. There were no cell phones to rely on then. By now, my business was thriving, so I splurged a little, sneaking in a three-day mini vacation to Jamaica. In 1986, after another mini vacation, the conversation about living in the United States surfaced, and we decided to get married the next day. My friends were shocked when I returned a married woman.

The wait for him to migrate to the United States ended earlier than expected. Finally, the visa was approved, and by the end of 1986, he emigrated to the United States. All was rosy-dozy in the beginning. I kept my evening job working at Zayre. However, more than ever before, I was bombarded with having a lot more on my plate than I imagined. I now had to provide for a husband who had not found a job yet.

However, through the help of a friend, he was soon referred for a job at the World Trade Center. The interview went well, and he was the final candidate. So finally, the financial help I so desperately needed was here. Though not really! Sometimes what you see is not what you get. People change when it is convenient for them.

In 1988, I became a mother to a beautiful baby girl with her father's looks and her mother's brain ~ so I was told!

My customers were patient and understanding. They adjusted their schedule to accommodate me, and I was able to work at home and go to the studio two days per week when I had to do a fitting.

It was comfortable working from home, as I had more time to spend with my daughter, giving me time to bond with her. Maybe it was God's answer to my prayers.

My home was now a working studio, and the place was becoming overcrowded. Before long, my home was no longer the happy place I had dreamed of. My household was beginning to unravel. Fear gripped me; I realized that I took a chance on someone who had ulterior motives.

Nevertheless, I found myself stuck, needing to make decisions independently and with little support.

What was I willing to give up? Who could I trust to share my deepest feelings of failure except for my pillow? So I would cry myself to sleep and hope for a better tomorrow.

Would I choose my business over him? Or was I going to go it alone? It was a tough decision, but I could always start another business. However, I knew that things had to change.

At the end of 1988, I sold the sewing machines, mannequins, bolts of fabric and coordinated a garment sample sale in the studio. It was heart-wrenching, but I had to make a choice. I never regretted my decision.

Self-love is never-ending;
pick up the broken pieces
and start over.

CHAPTER 8

Single Parent

I landed the title of "a single parent" years before the divorce decree was settled, signed, and the ink on the paper dried.

I remember my daughter's birth in 1988 at 2:42 am in St. Luke's Hospital in Manhattan on a chilly, windy morning. Feeling hopeless and alone, I quickly looked at her picture in my wallet and was overwhelmed with joy. I knew I had to keep going.

Arrangements were in place for customers to meet with my seamstress while I was home. I planned on taking a few weeks off, and then I would work from home. The business was now dissolved, and I became accustomed to being home with my daughter. However, I still had customers who requested my service.

Hopefully, the money I saved would carry me through, as I planned on staying home for six months. By then, I would have referred my customers to another designer. Unfortunately, business was slower than usual, and my full-time job at Zayre was in jeopardy. The company was terminating workers as they relocated the warehouse out of state. Was this the answer to my prayer?

My early years of motherhood consisted of challenges for which I was not prepared: getting up many hours earlier than usual, making sure enough feeding bottles, changing clothes, and Pampers were ready, and packing all into the baby bag, getting dressed myself, then off to the babysitter.

I received my termination notice from Zayre in the mail. After dropping off my daughter at the babysitter the following day, I went to the unemployment office to submit my claim. As a dislocated worker, I was eligible for unemployment, and it was required that I participate in a work-based training program. This program included learning secretarial and computer skills and typing to update my current skills for the job market.

As a single parent, I had only me, myself and I to depend on. I had to put my wish list on hold for now. My day begins with, and ended with Mackie and taking care of my daughter needs. It was a position I did not take lightly, putting everything else on hold. I succeeded in fulfilling my goal of becoming a fashion designer in New York, as I know I did my best.

As she got older and ready for pre-kindergarten, my daughter would pick out her clothes, already fashionable, even if the piece of clothing did not match or was color coordinated. We always looked forward to going to Cookies children's store on Jamaica Avenue to purchase the cutest dresses and play outfits. Spring was her favorite season as we would dress up to perfection in our hot pink spring coat to meet the easter bunny and hunt for easter eggs.

There was no shortage of activities; we were involved in local and national children beauty pageants, achievement pageants, traveling to compete in state pageants, national competition at Disney in Florida, dance classes and company class competitions, even learning to play the Caribbean Pan instrument. Our lives were joyful, adventurous, educational, and spiritual.

Trading the life I had was never an option, and as my daughter blossomed into her teen years, I worried if she would still be what I expected her to grow up to be. Those were the years I prayed more than I ever did, as outside influences were wreaking havoc. Yet, I held firm to my faith and trusted the counsel of those in positions to help me. I put aside the stigma that seeking help was shameful. We both overcame the rough times as I stood firm with a "tough love" attitude.

High school to college was more tolerable; my daughter now understood it was best to follow the rules. I now could breathe easily but did not let go of the reins. I have no regrets as I did my part as a parent: No pain, no gain.

Single parenting is challenging;
the sacrifice is huge,
but the rewards are much greater.

CHAPTER 9

Nothing But Hard Work

Growing up, I watched my grandparents working diligently to achieve their goals and provide luxury for the family to live a comfortable life. As a result, I was no stranger to hard work. I spent my childhood watching my grandmother plant vegetables in the backyard and get up early in the wee hours of the morning to collect the walnuts that had fallen from the tree overnight to place on the veranda ledge to dry as soon as the sun began to shine.

Thus, I was never afraid of hard work, or shy away from the challenges of working hard. We raised chickens at my grandparents' house in St. Andrew, Jamaica. We grew vegetables and any other fruit that the climate allowed us to plant, such as the ackee tree that the "long tone man," as my mother called the thief who had scaled the barbed wired fence, to enter the back yard to climb the ackee tree helping himself to what he did not plant. My favorite trees were the mango trees, bearing a juicy, delicious fruit of several types of mangoes that would fall from the tree once they were ripe and ready for eating.

My work ethic began at the age of 14 when during the summer, I worked at the Bustamante Industrial Union (BITU) on Duke Street in Kingston, Jamaica. I was responsible for answering the telephones and filing. The following summer, I worked at the National Water Commission in New Kingston, Jamaica. My position here was similar to those at the Bustamante Industrial Trade Union (BITU). I also learned how to respond to customers who came to pay their water bills before shutting their water off.

After graduating from Immaculate Conception high school, I worked at several part-time jobs in New Kingston as a data entry clerk before being employed in a permanent full-time position at Datatron, where I remained until migrating to the United States.

Once I began living in the United States, I did not change my work ethic but worked harder. From 1991 to 1921, I worked as a public servant, which allowed me to be kind personally and professionally. I earned accolades, but I learned from a stranger the impact of kindness when stranded at the airport. Without her, I don't know where I would be today. I succeeded in my quest, fulfilling my goal of becoming a fashion designer in New York City; I know I did my best.

Seize the opportunity to be kind;
it builds character.

CHAPTER 10

Achieving Goals

I have peace of mind as I have never forgotten my roots. I did my best; this is my success. I have tried to achieve the goals I set for myself, although sometimes not in the order I expected. When I refer to my long-term goals, my expected term is five to ten years of hard work.

The goals I have accomplished since migrating to the United States are many. I survived through struggles, heartbreak, cold winter months, and sleepless nights. I have so much to be thankful for and, to be proud of ~ my successes. I have taken the time to list a summary of each accomplished goal.

1. Migrating to the United States: It was overwhelming. I listened and learned, following the steps of others to find employment in the United States of America. This move was a challenging endeavor but worth the effort.
2. Getting a good-paying job: I was willing to go after my desired career and put in the necessary pavement pounding in unknown territories. I prepared myself to start from the bottom.

3. Earning a US high school diploma: The challenge of returning to school to earn a high school diploma in the United States helped me save college tuition. I was able to take my high school classes online as I had no desire to sit in a classroom.

4. Attending college: The rigors of applying to colleges was overwhelming. The application process was lengthy and tedious. The fear of rejection if not accepted was traumatic.

5. Having my own business: Searching for and finding a suitable place for a fashion design studio.

6. Becoming a designer in New York City: This was not easy without the skills and experience. Continuing education in a trade school or college is necessary.

7. Getting married: This was a big decision that needed time to think before consenting. You could live to regret your action.

8. Raising my daughter on my own: A big decision with no regrets. The choice is up to the person and willingness to go alone, putting your wish list on hold.

9. Going back to college: In some cases, it is crucial always to finish what you start never leave any stone unturned. Taking the risk is worth it in capturing new ideas.

10. Getting a professional job in academia: Learn as you go along, as we only have one mouth but two ears to listen. Must prepare yourself for skilled employment. A degree surely helps.

I have accomplished the goals I set for myself. My unfilled goal of retiring continues. I am currently enjoying the peace and quiet of taking one day at a time. Therefore, there is no such thing as retirement in my book. "I just have a new career." There is much to be done before I leave this earth to stop now! Retirement to the author means: I get to choose what I want to do, when I want it's done, making everything worthwhile. I want to fulfil my purpose and not just waiting for the breath to leave the body. Each life has a purpose. Plan, live and enjoy your best life. Thank you for the opportunity to share My Fashionable Journey.

The End of This Journey

In 1969, I was stranded at an airport in another country not knowing where place to go. A stranger asked to share a taxi with me and offered me a place to stay for the night. If that had been you, would you accept?

Life comes with unexpected turns, even great disappointments, but mixed in them all are some serendipitous occasions that can only be considered a God-moment. Depending on the timing and location and your emotions, it just might be time to follow your instincts and acknowledge your gut feeling that something on the inside of you is compelling you to move forward. *Find your purpose?* Say a prayer for divine intervention and protection then go forth.

Always know if accomplishing your goal is keeping you up at night tossing and turning, then it's worth taking the time and effort you invest. But trust your judgment, be careful and stay conscious. Further, if you have no money and no place to stay for the night, only a kind and caring person would be willing to take a chance to put you up. Trust is not something you see; it's something you feel, you'll know. There will be a feeling of peace, even amid concern or even a little fear. It's the beginning of the journey you never saw coming; it may be worth it.

In 1992, Commissioner Josephine Nieves and the City of New York chose me as an honoree and alumni of the Job Training Partnership Act. I joined Mayor Dinkins at the official event celebrating the outstanding achievements of determination and integrity to gain employment by the many courageous people who call the City of New York home.

My life is fashioned from the skills and values I learned from family members. I stand on their shoulders; it gives me the opportunity to soar!

Standing On The Shoulders Of Giants.

THE CITY OF NEW YORK
DEPARTMENT OF EMPLOYMENT
220 CHURCH STREET
NEW YORK, N. Y. 10013

JOSEPHINE NIEVES
Commissioner

August 4, 1992

Ms. Cheryl Powell
87-70 173rd Street - Apt. 2K
Jamaica, NY 11432

Dear Ms. Powell:

I am delighted to inform you that you have been selected as an honoree in celebration of the New York City Department's annual JTPA Alumni Week. On behalf Commissioner Josephine Nieves, we congratulate you on your outstanding achievements with the Family Institute. You should be very proud of your success. You are an example for all those who are working to be the best they can be.

To observe this special occasion, the New York City Department of Employment cordially invites you to our JTPA Awards Ceremony to be held on August 13th at 10:00 A.M. in the Board of Estimate Chambers at City Hall.

We hope you and your family and friends will join us for the ceremony. JTPA alumni are New Yorkers who have turned their lives around. Your experiences with JTPA create powerful stories of determination and integrity. We invite you to join Mayor Dinkins and our Commissioner Josephine Nieves in the festivities.

Please confirm your attendance by August 7th by calling 433-6279. See you there.

Sincerely,

Walther Delgado

I believe all things are possible
and are grounded in determination and perseverance.
I learned about having faith at an early age
from Mamma, my Jamaican grandmother.

Photograph credits:

All photographs are from the author's collection.
About the Author Bio photo: Jeff Smith - ReflectionsNYC
Newspaper clippings photographs: Carib News 1985